We the People

The Constitution and You

THE RIGHT TO BEAR ARMS

by Paul J. Deegan

Abdo & Daughters
Minneapolis

Published by Abdo & Daughters, 6537 Cecilia Circle, Bloomington, Minnesota 55435

Library bound edition distributed by Rockbottom Books, Pentagon Tower, P.O. Box 36036, Minneapolis, Minnesota 55435

Library of Congress Number: 87-071088   ISBN: 0-939179-24-5

Cover illustration by Elaine Wadsworth

Consultants:

Phyllis R. Abbott
Ph.D. — University of Wisconsin (Madison)
Professor of History
Mankato State University
Mankato, Minnesota

Bailey W. Blethen
J.D. — University of Minnesota Law School
Partner in law firm of Blethen, Gage & Krause
Mankato, Minnesota

Lewis H. Croce
Ph.D. — University of Maryland
Professor of History
Mankato State University
Mankato, Minnesota

Milepost 55 column by Betty Nelson in March 13, 1987, The Free Press. Copyright © 1987 by The Free Press. Used with permission of Mankato (Minnesota) Free Press Co., Division of Ottaway Newspapers, Inc.

The first 10 Amendments to the United States Constitution

The Bill of Rights

AMENDMENT 1

Congress shall make no law respecting an establishment of religion, or prohibiting the free exercise thereof; or abridging the freedom of speech, or of the press; or the right of the people peaceably to assemble, and to petition the government for a redress of grievances.

AMENDMENT 2

A well-regulated militia being necessary to the security of a free State, the right of the people to keep and bear arms shall not be infringed.

AMENDMENT 3

No soldier shall, in time of peace be quartered in any house without the consent of the owner, nor in time of war, but in a manner to be prescribed by law.

AMENDMENT 4

The right of the people to be secure in their persons, houses, papers and effects, against unreasonable searches and seizures, shall not be violated, and no warrants shall issue but upon probable cause, supported by oath or affirmation, and particularly describing the place to be searched, and the persons or things to be seized.

AMENDMENT 5

No person shall be held to answer for a capital or otherwise infamous crime, unless on a presentment or indictment of a grand jury, except in cases arising in the land or naval forces, or in the militia, when in actual service in time of war or public danger; nor shall any person be subject for the same offense to be twice put in jeopardy of life or limb; nor shall be compelled in any criminal case to be a witness against himself, nor be deprived of life, liberty, or property, without due process of law; nor shall private property be taken for public use, without just compensation.

AMENDMENT 6

In all criminal prosecutions, the accused shall enjoy the right to a speedy and public trial, by an impartial jury of the State and district wherein the crime shall have been committed, which district shall have been previously ascertained by law, and to be informed of the nature and cause of the accusation; to be confronted with the witnesses against him; to have compulsory process of obtaining witnesses in his favor, and to have the assistance of counsel for his defense.

AMENDMENT 7

In suits at common law, where the value in controversy shall exceed twenty dollars, the right of trial by jury, shall be preserved, and no fact tried by a jury shall be otherwise reexamined in any court of the United States than according to the rules of the common law.

AMENDMENT 8

Excessive bail shall not be required, nor excessive fines imposed, nor cruel and unusual punishments inflicted.

AMENDMENT 9

The enumeration in the Constitution of certain rights shall not be construed to deny or disparage others retained by the people.

AMENDMENT 10

The powers not delegated to the United States by the Constitution, nor prohibited by it to the States, are reserved to the States respectively, or to the people.

"We the People of the United States . . . establish this CONSTITUTION for the United States of America."

When the Founding Fathers wrote the Constitution in 1787 popular opinion opposed a standing army. State militias — citizen-soldiers — were favored.

So two years later when the first 10 Amendments to the Constitution, the Bill of Rights, was drafted, the Founding Fathers involved in this task included an Amendment that dealt with militias.

They were not thinking about burglars lurking in someone's basement when they drafted the 2nd Amendment.

However, when Americans in 1987 talk about the 2nd Amendment, they sometimes are thinking about guns and burglars.

Say it's the middle of the night. You're awakened from sleep in your upstairs bedroom by the sound of shattering glass.

Still groggy upon awakening, it takes you a few seconds to figure out what caused you to wake up. Oh yes, the sound of breaking glass.

Could there be a burglar in your basement?

You suddenly remember that you're home alone. Your parents are spending the night out of town.

You turn on a bedside light.

What was that noise? Is there an intruder in your house?

Could be.

What to do? You're scared. Your mind is racing.

You remember your father keeps a rifle in his bedroom closet. But that's down the hall, and you don't have any idea whether or not the gun is loaded.

Should you get the gun?

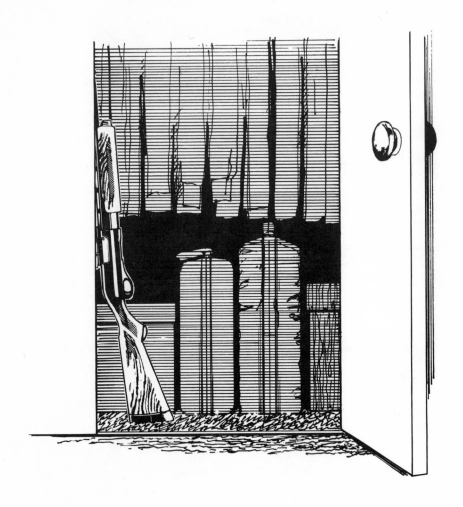

Your mind is still racing . . . what's happening — if anything — downstairs?

Then your eyes fall on your phone. On it in large letters is an emergency number. You thought it was dumb when your mother put the label on the phone.

Right now it seems like a great idea!

You dial the number. An operator at the switchboard in the local public safety building takes your call.

Speaking softly, and hurriedly, you say you think someone has broken into your house. The operator asks your address.

As you give it, the message is being relayed to police patrol cars. The one closest to your neighborhood responds immediately. A patrolman gets out of his car at your house, hand on his service revolver.

A scene similar to this one is played out each night in an American city.

However, 200 years ago it was a different America.

There were less than four million people, almost all living in 13 states close to the Eastern seaboard. Georgia was the state farthest to the west.

When the Bill of Rights to the Constitution of the United States was written in 1789, there was no emergency number to call. There wasn't even a telephone. Nor was there a light to turn on.

Nor was there a policeman to answer a summons. Life was not the same in the 1780s as it is today.

Then most citizens lived in rural areas. They were on their own in terms of protecting their homes and property. Even in larger towns — Philadelphia with some 40,000 people was the largest city — there was no organized police force as we know it today.

There also was no national standing army. The Continental Army had been hastily formed to fight the Revolutionary War. When the war was over, the regular troops and the officers went back to whatever they did before taking up arms to fight the British.

The commanding officer of the Continental Army, George Washington, was serving as the new nation's first President when the Bill of Rights was produced in the first Congress to meet under the recently ratified Constitution.

At the time the only thing resembling an army was a "militia" which each state was expected to maintain and train. A militia was formed by citizen-soldiers. They did not go to basic training, and drilled infrequently.

It was thought at the time that a militia was all that was needed in normal times to enforce the laws and defend the country.

"Militia all that was needed."

The states too were forbidden to have standing armies without the specific consent of Congress.

The Constitution as originally adopted gave overall responsibility for a state's militia to Congress. This authority was contained in Article I. States were to

H.A.Ogden.

·1779· IV ·1783·
INFANTRY · CONTINENTAL · ARMY ·

appoint officers of a militia and had the responsibility for training these very part-time soldiers. The method of training was to be set forth by Congress.

Today millions of men and women and billions of dollars are involved in maintaining the armed forces of the United States.

There are well-organized, uniformed police forces on the state, county, and local levels.

The regular and reserve armed forces have and use guns of every sort — handguns, rifles, machine guns, and much larger guns on motorized vehicles and ships. Police forces also have a variety of guns which they are trained to use. Police officers generally carry pistols.

But your average citizen doesn't walk around with a rifle or handgun in the 1980s. Today there are federal, state, and local laws regarding guns. There are laws regulating the purchase, possession, and use of guns. Some deal with registration of guns.

Few people in this country express concern about people owning shotguns and rifles for use in hunting or target shooting. Therefore most of the laws apply to handguns, automatic weapons, and modified long guns. There are laws, however, regarding the transportation of long guns, including ones forbidding carrying an uncased or loaded shotgun or rifle in a vehicle.

Some laws carry serious penalties, such as making it a federal crime to possess an automatic weapon.

There are, of course, exceptions for police and military forces.

There are federal and state laws which increase the penalty to someone who commits a crime while using a gun.

A person convicted of a serious crime cannot have a gun.

Today, the government certainly doesn't care if you don't own a gun.

That was not the case in the early days of our country. In the 1600s, long before the Constitution was written, colonialists who were adult males generally were expected to have guns.

The militia system of that time was based on the principle that men had an obligation both to have guns and to assist in whatever defense of their town or area might be necessary.

This system followed the practice in England at the time.

By the 1780s, some states had adopted this system as part of their state laws establishing militias. In Massachusetts, militia men were required to have a "good fire arm." In Virginia militia men had to have "a good, clean musket" and "a good bayonet."

A musket was a smoothbore shoulder gun. A bayonet is a knife adapted to fit the end of a rifle.

A fight between soldiers in those days often meant face-to-face fighting where the bayonet was more important than the bullets the gun could fire.

It was this atmosphere with which James Madison and his fellow citizens were familiar in 1789. Madison wrote the first nine amendments in the Bill of Rights.

The second of these says:

"A well-regulated militia, being necessary to the security of a free state, the right of the people to keep and bear arms, shall not be infringed."

This language today means different things to different Americans when they talk about "the right . . . to keep and bear arms." Talk about rights is common among Americans. They usually are referring to the basic liberties protected by the Constitution in the Bill of Rights.

Perhaps no language in the Bill of Rights creates as much emotion as the right cited in the 2nd Amendment.

This is in no small part due to incidents such as one described by a newspaper columnist. "I had heard the story," she wrote, about how a 20-year-old man "had been shot to death" in a motel parking lot in Florida in 1983.

Writing in 1987, she said:

"The shot had been fired by a man with a name he (the dead man) never knew, for reasons impossible to understand. Such a violent end seemed somehow remote." The story, according to the columnist, "is true and tragic and unnecessary."

David, she wrote, was a Vero Beach minister's son. While on a weekend outing just before leaving home for his second year of college, she said, he and two other young men drove south to Fort Pierce to hear a rock band play in a motel bar to which they had never been before.

The night spot, the columnist wrote, "had the reputation of being sometimes a rowdy place." The three stayed at the bar for an hour, listening to the music and having a beer or two before returning home.

"In the parking lot of the motel they were accosted by three local men in their 30s who'd been drinking at a birthday dinner there. The older men taunted the younger ones with obscenities. This was documented at a trial later on."

"It would have been merely an unpleasant interlude had David not discovered he'd left his car keys in the lounge. Returning to the parking area with the keys, he found his two friends in a name-calling fistfight with the three locals. He joined the fray.

"Suddenly, one of the men pulled a gun from the top of the boot he was wearing and fired three times at point-blank range. The first shot killed David instantly. The second shattered the jaw of one of his friends. The third tore through the brain of the other."

The other two injured men lived, she reported. "The one faced years of reconstructive surgery on his shattered jaw. The other, with a bullet in his skull, never recovered his memory or his intellect. . .

"Three young men, their normal lives ruined beyond recall. Three shots fired by a man they'd never met, for reasons known only to him."

At a trial on charges related to the shooting, the columnist wrote, the man who fired the shots "testified that he always kept his gun in the top of his boot, 'put it there the same way I put my billfold in my back pocket.' "

The assailant was never convicted in regard to David's death, the columnist said, but was convicted of another charge related to the shootings, "served a short term in prison," and is now out of prison.

"The young man with the reconstructed jaw is back in college," the columnist said. The other injured man "is doing odd jobs — yard work" in his hometown.

Incidents such as this inevitably lead to discussions about gun control.

The topic can bring about a heated argument.

For instance, a reader wrote to the newspaper in which the column about the Florida shootings appeared. In that letter to the editor, the reader said:

"Gun laws don't do anything except make trouble for a law-abiding voter."

Many people do not want the government at any level interfering with their desire to own and keep guns.

This viewpoint may be a reflection of some people's overall suspicion and distrust of government.

Gun control is a factor in elections in this country. Politicians can be elected and defeated on the basis of their views on gun control.

One of the largest and most effective lobbying organizations in the country is the National Rifle Association. This organization does not like restrictions on the possession of guns. They make their viewpoint known to lawmakers.

On the other side are those who favor stricter laws with regard to handguns.

Those who favor stricter laws regulating handguns say their goal includes making the country "a safer, saner place." They generally maintain that such laws make it more difficult for people who want to commit crimes to obtain such guns.

Sarah Brady is the wife of James Brady, President Ronald Reagan's press secretary. Mr. Brady was seriously injured when he was shot by a man apparently trying to kill the President. President Reagan and two officers also were wounded.

Mrs. Brady says that had a federal law effective in 1987 been in effect in 1981, the assailant ". . . would not have purchased the gun. . ." used to shoot the President and her husband.

Those who oppose such gun control laws disagree with Mrs. Brady. They argue that somebody who wants to commit a crime will find a way to get a gun no matter what the law says. They say gun control laws only restrict the law-abiding citizen from pursuing his desires.

Those on either side of the gun control issue approach the issue with much fervor. It is an important issue to them.

However, it is a subject which has never been a significant issue in Constitutional law. There are no really significant Supreme Court decisions on this issue.

"No really significant decisions."

Interpretations vary with regard to what the 2nd Amendment actually grants Americans. The discussion has been going on for generations.

Still there are many persons who have invoked the right to bear arms in asking courts of appeal to review their convictions. However, the courts have not treated this issue as one of our fundamental rights.

In fact, it is one right which has never been formally "incorporated" against the states.

When the Bill of Rights went into effect in 1791, they applied only to the federal government. They did not apply to the states. States had laws which limited rights protected by the Bill of Rights.

Not until the decision in 1925 in *Gitlow versus New York* did the Supreme Court impose the Bill of Rights' guarantees upon the states.

The court in this decision used the 14th Amendment, which went into effect in 1868, as the vehicle for prohibiting states from interfering with the protection of the basic rights set out in the Bill of Rights. This process of applying the Bill of Rights to the states through the 14th Amendment is known in legal terms as "incorporation".

Some scholars say that because of incorporation, the 14th Amendment is our "second bill of rights."

The Supreme Court said in a 1939 decision, *United States versus Miller,* which dealt with the right to bear arms that the 2nd Amendment is a check on the powers of Congress, not the states. The 2nd Amendment is not likely to be applied against the states via the 14th Amendment.

In the Miller case, two men, Jack Miller and Frank Layton, had been accused by a Federal District Court in Arkansas of violating the National Firearms Act. They were charged with transporting a sawed-off shotgun across state lines — from Oklahoma to Arkansas — without registration and without the necessary permit.

The men asked a court in Arkansas, the trial court, to dismiss the charge because, they said, the National Firearms Act violated their rights under the Constitution.

It was unconstitutional, they said, because it offended the 2nd Amendment guarantee of the right to bear arms.

The trial court agreed with them. It dismissed the complaint. The federal government appealed that decision to the United States Supreme Court.

The Supreme Court's decision would relate the Constitution to you . . .

Was the arrest of these two men an interference with their "right to bear arms?"

What did the high court say about this right which stirs so much emotion.

The 2nd Amendment, the Supreme Court said, was designed for that period of time when states were expected to maintain their own militias. And, according to the court, the amendment was based on the fact that members of a militia were expected to supply their own weapons for combat.

For the defendants to have been successful in their argument that their right to bear arms was being violated, they would have had to offer certain evidence at their trial. They would have had to show that the sawed-off shotgun was in fact part of their activities as a member of a state militia.

In the absence of evidence showing this was true, the court said ". . . it cannot be said that the 2nd Amendment . . . guarantees the right to keep and bear such an instrument (the shotgun) . . ." Nor, then, the court held, does the National Firearms Act violate the amendment.

The Supreme Court overturned the trial court decision and returned the case to the trial court.

One of the things courts of appeal consider when reviewing cases is the legislative history with regard to the law or laws in question. In *United States versus Miller,* the Supreme Court cited a good deal of such history to show why they came to the decision they reached.

It probably would be very difficult to find any legislative history that supports a totally different notion, the notion that the 2nd Amendment is intended to permit people to carry around sawed-off shotguns or other weapons intended to be used against people for purposes having nothing to do with a "well-regulated militia."

In another gun control case arising 45 years later, a Chicago man challenged that city's law regulating handguns. The Chicago law regulated possession and registration. The man, Jerome Sklar, used several arguments, among them that the law violated his 2nd Amendment right to bear arms.

This case never went to the Supreme Court. However, a federal court of appeals said the Chicago law did not violate "any federal Constitutional right to bear arms."

It also referred to the matter of incorporation. It said the 2nd Amendment ". . . regulates only the activities of the federal government — not those of the states or their subdivisions (such as the city of Chicago)."

"2nd Amendment . . . regulates only activities of federal government."

So an issue about which many Americans feel very strongly, the right to "keep and bear arms," hasn't been a major issue in terms of how the Bill of Rights applies to gun ownership and use.

And to date anyway, whatever right is granted by the 2nd Amendment does not apply to state and local governments.